The Lord is My Shepherd

The Psalm of Victorious Life

Robert C. McQuilkin

Columbia International University

Columbia, South Carolina

The Lord is My Shepherd: The Psalm of Victorious Life

Updated edition
Copyright © 2014 by Columbia International University

7435 Monticello Rd.
Columbia, SC 29203
www.ciu.edu

Columbia International University exists to train men and women from a
biblical world view to impact the nations with the message of Christ through
service in the marketplace, missions and the local church.

Editing, Cover and interior book design by Kelly Smith, Tallgrass Media.
Cover photo from iStockphoto, used by permission.

Scripture quotations are from The Holy Bible, English Standard Version®
(ESV®), copyright © 2001 by Crossway, a publishing ministry of Good News
Publishers. Used by permission. All rights reserved.

Ninth printing.
First Printing: 1938

ISBN-13: 978-1-939074-03-4

Contents

Introduction to the Series

Dr. Robert C. McQuilkin served as the first president of Columbia International University, then named Columbia Bible College (CBC) for 29 years; 1923-1952. He served Christ and the Church as a magazine editor, a dynamic speaker, and a prolific writer. But he also had a deep passion to teach. During his tenure as president, he taught Romans, John, Daniel and Revelation, Progress of Doctrine, Hermeneutics and other courses. The books in this series spilled over from those courses and from popular sermons he preached across the nation.

Dr. McQuilkin expressed the vision for a biblical university that outlines my own service as president: "Neither a Bible institute nor a liberal arts college, Columbia Bible College offers a curriculum with the spiritual advantages of the former, and the cultural advantages of the latter."

After Dr. McQuilkin's sudden death, G. Allen Fleece led the school in its move to CIU's present location. His plans for expansion laid the foundation for Dr. McQuilkin's son, Robertson, who became president in 1968 when Dr. Fleece returned to his first love of evangelism.

Robertson McQuilkin left the church planting work he loved in Japan to lead CIU from 1968 to 1990. Robertson, like his dad, writes, preaches, and teaches. His books on hermeneutics, world evangelization, ethics, and the Holy Spirit continue in print and are used by schools and ministries around the world.

I invite you to join us in revisiting our rich heritage of the written works of Robert and Robertson McQuilkin. After all, together they provided leadership to CIU for over 50 years.

Within their writings, you will notice themes that form CIU's core values:

- Biblical Authority: The authority of Scripture as the defining rule for belief and practice.
- Victorious Christian Life: The victory in Christ that every Christian can experience through the filling of the Spirit.
- Prayer and Faith: The consistent practice by every Christian of personal witness to God's saving work in Christ.
- World Evangelization: The alignment of every Christian with God's heart for those around the world who have never heard the gospel.
- Evangelical Unity: Protecting the core truths of the faith, while seeking evangelical unity on all nonessentials.

We still live by these five core values as a school and to revisit them again in these books solidifies our commitment to them. We look back to remember and to underscore the importance of remaining tethered to our foundations, while exercising relevance in a dynamic, global community.

We look forward, until Christ returns, to serving His church by educating people from a biblical worldview to impact the nations with the message of Christ.

Dr. Bill Jones
President, Columbia International University
www.ciu.edu

Foreword

Why re-publish the writings of one who died more than a half century ago? Well, some would say, because they are classics by a major Christian author. But there's more.

Ninety years after their founding, very few institutions accurately reflect all the core values the founder held. But the grace of God through the creative genius of my father, Robert C. McQuilkin, has done just that. He was involved with initiating many movements and institutions. Some have morphed into something different than he envisioned. Some have disappeared. But the institution he poured his life into — Columbia Bible College — continues to this day in the vision and path he laid down, known today as Columbia International University.

Perhaps the enduring impact of his writing results in part, not only for its biblical fidelity on the God-intended life, but because his writing was signed and sealed by the life of the author. As I testified at his memorial service in 1952, "I know my father has sinned because 'all have sinned.' But I want you to know that for 25 years living in his house, I've never known him to fail."

It is fitting that this treasure trove should once again be made available to the CIU family and, as in the beginning, far beyond.

J. Robertson McQuilkin
President Emeritus
Columbia International University
August 2012

Photo of Robertson McQuilkin with his father in the 1950s.

Original Foreword by the Author

Without a rival among the songs that reach the heart, the twenty-third Psalm is the greatest poem ever penned in any language. It reigns supreme in circles of highest culture and in the humble homes of the lowly. It sounds all the chords of human experience, from depths of sorrow to heights of joy, taking us beside waters of stillness and into the strife of the enemy's country, covering all the days of our life down here, and reaching into eternity. And all this is compassed in just fifty-five words in the Hebrew original.

Do we know this "Psalm of Life"? Some of the most gifted writers and preachers and poets have illumined for us the glories of the twenty-third Psalm. This exposition is not an attempt to unfold the wonders or the beauty of the psalm, but is intended to help Christians to enter into a life of victory by believing the gracious revelation of the Psalm of Victorious Life. Thus may we become sheep of his pasture in whom others may read the message of the Shepherd Psalm.

Psalm 23

English Standard Version (ESV)

[1] The Lord is my shepherd; I shall not want.
   [2] He makes me lie down in green pastures.
He leads me beside still waters.
   [3] He restores my soul.
He leads me in paths of righteousness
      for his name's sake.
[4] Even though I walk through the valley of the shadow of death,
      I will fear no evil,
for you are with me;
      your rod and your staff,
      they comfort me.
[5] You prepare a table before me
      in the presence of my enemies;
you anoint my head with oil;
      my cup overflows.
[6] Surely goodness and mercy shall follow me
      all the days of my life,
and I shall dwell in the house of the Lord forever.

Chapter 1

The Psalm of Victorious Life

Have you ever read the twenty-third Psalm? You quickly answer, with gladness, and with some surprise that the question should be asked: "Why, I know the twenty-third Psalm by heart."

There are those who have been able to recite the twenty-third Psalm since they were three years old, yet have never really read it. They know the words of the psalm, but they do not know it "by heart."

The twenty-third Psalm is the best known chapter in the Bible — and the least understood. It is the best loved chapter of the Bible — and the least believed.

A dear Christian mother, a sweet woman of about sixty, came to the writer at the close of a meeting, and with troubled face and voice, cried: "Oh, that life of victory! That is what I need. If I could only have that joy and peace in my heart." She then poured out history of the troubles in the home, because of the unworthy conduct of the man who had married her beautiful Christian daughter.

"Have you ever read the thirty-seventh Psalm?" I asked.

Her face lit up: "Yes! That is my favorite Psalm! I know it by heart."

"What is the first word of the thirty-seventh Psalm?"

I expected her to say: "Fret not." She answered accurately, "Fret." That was the only part of the thirty-seventh Psalm she knew by heart! She was fretting much of the time. She repeated the first sentence of the psalm: "Fret not yourself because of evil doers." I asked her who was fretting her; she said it was this young man, and proceeded to tell

other things about the troubles in the home. After repeating the opening words of the thirty-seventh Psalm several times, the meaning of
the words, "Fret not yourself," finally dawned upon her.

"Oh," she cried, "you mean that *I'm* the one that's doing it, and all
the time I thought it was that man."

Others may be the occasion of our worry, but none can fret us
except ourselves. I was not sure that this dear Christian really learned
the thirty-seventh Psalm by heart on that day. But years afterwards I
was telling the story in a meeting hundreds of miles removed from
this Christian's home. A friend of hers from the same city was present
and told me the good news that her friend *had* learned that day the
secret of the peace that passes understanding.

Moreover, the son-in-law became an earnest, useful Christian, and
the home was a happy home.

But what has this beautiful working of God in the life of that
Christian to do with the twenty-third Psalm? It is an illustration of the
fact that it is possible to know the words of the twenty-third Psalm,
and yet not to believe them. For to believe the twenty-third Psalm is to
live a life of victory, a life of joy and peace, a life triumphant in prayer,
in Bible study, in service.

This Shepherd Psalm is the real "Psalm of Life." The twenty-second
Psalm, with its opening cry, "My God, my God, why have you forsaken
me?" has been called the Psalm of "the Good Shepherd," who lays down
his life for the sheep (John 10:11). The twenty-fourth Psalm with its
triumphant, "Lift up your heads, O gates … that the King of glory
may come in," has been called the Psalm of "the Chief Shepherd," who
ascended in triumph and who is coming again in glory (I Peter 5:4).
The twenty-third Psalm is the Psalm of present resurrection life, and
has been called the Psalm of "the Great Shepherd"; "Now may the God

of peace who brought again from the dead our Lord Jesus, the great shepherd of the sheep, by the blood of the eternal covenant, equip you with everything good that you may do his will, working in us that which is pleasing in his sight, through Jesus Christ" (Hebrews 13:20, 21). The twenty-third Psalm has been called the valley between two mountains, Mount Calvary on one side, and Mount Olivet on the other.

Let us read the psalm together, and enter into its secret.

"The Lord is my Shepherd; I shall not want." I shall not want what? The answer is found in Psalm 34:10: "... but those who seek the Lord lack no good thing." Because the Lord is my Shepherd (whatever the rich meaning of that may be), I shall not lack any good. The other five verses of this psalm describe, in terms of the middle-eastern shepherd and his sheep, the good things that the Lord provides.

If one were asked to name the most wonderful allegory written in the English language, the answer might well be *Pilgrim's Progress.* In my opinion, the twenty-third Psalm is the greatest allegory ever written. The expression "The Lord is my Shepherd," is a figure of speech, called a metaphor. An allegory is often defined as an extended metaphor. The natural figure and the spiritual reality it sets forth are linked together in each sentence. So this psalm speaks directly of the Lord and his people, but does it in terms of the shepherd and his sheep. The form of the beautiful parable of the sheep-fold in John 10 is different from this. In John 10, verses one to five, all the words apply to the literal sheepfold, and sheep, and shepherd, although the Lord is giving the picture to set forth his own relation with believers.

Chapter 2

What the Shepherd Does

L et us keep in mind this figurative language as we read through Psalm twenty-three, first considering verses two to six, then returning to the opening statement, "The Lord is my Shepherd," which is the key that unlocks the rich treasures of the psalm of victorious life.

"He makes me lie down in green pastures: he leads me beside still waters." The Lord is my Shepherd: I shall not want the supply of every material and spiritual need. He is the bread of life. He gives the water of life. The primary reference here is to the supply of material needs, as in the Lord's prayer: "Give us this day our daily bread." Yet one can never think of the Lord Jesus supplying bread for the body, without remembering that this material bread is a symbol of the living bread. He supplies every need.

Have you ever worried about the supply of material needs? Do you have perfect peace now about the meeting of the material needs of yourself, of all your loved ones, of the Christian work with which you are associated? If you do not have that peace, you are not believing the message of the twenty-third Psalm.

"He restores my soul." The weak or wounded or weary or wandering sheep needs the shepherd to restore his life. The Lord is our Shepherd: He forgives our sin, cleansing us from all unrighteousness; he refreshes us when weary and encourages us when cast down. Are you discouraged now, or weary, or disappointed, sick at heart, or tired in spirit? You need restoration. Is the Shepherd restoring your soul? If not, there is a glorious message of victory for you in this psalm of life.

"He leads me in paths of righteousness for his name's sake." The shepherd leads the sheep in right paths. The Lord is my Shepherd: I shall not want guidance. Our Shepherd guides us into right paths, and He does it not because we are worthy but "for his name's sake." Have you been troubled about the question of guidance, in great things or in small? Are you sure now that you are in the right path? If not, will you believe now that the Lord is your Shepherd?

"Even though I walk through the valley of the shadow of death, I will fear no evil." The Lord is my Shepherd: I shall not want deliverance from every fear of any evil. Nearly always this verse is quoted as referring to death, and is used to give comfort at death and assurance of the presence of the Lord to carry the believer through the dark valley. It does give such comfort and assurance. But the twenty-third Psalm is a psalm of resurrection life, and the reference here is not to death. There is no dark valley for a Christian who dies. There may, indeed, be pain and suffering and darkness before death. But our Lord's promise is very sure, that they who believe in Him shall never see death (John 8:51, 52).

When a believer dies, his spirit is so instantaneously in the presence of the Lord that he may feel with Paul that he knows not whether he is in the body or out of the body (Phil. 1:23; 2 Cor. 12 :1-4). In any case, it is very certain that there is no dark valley for any believer. Christ has conquered death. The body does not rest in the power of death until the resurrection. Yet in a true sense a believer never tastes of death. The bitterness has all been taken out.

Those who are sorrowing because of the death of loved ones are they who pass through the valley of the shadow of death, or the valley of deep darkness. Any time of sorrow or grief or trouble is a valley of the shadow of death. The shepherd may take his sheep through a dangerous valley, with rough rocks and muddy roads and dismal swamps. As one has beautifully suggested, the shepherd never does this unless it be necessary in leading the sheep to rich green pastures on the other side. So with our Shepherd. He never suffers us to be tested above that we are able (1 Cor. 10:13). He permits tears and sorrow only that through them He may bring us rich spiritual blessings that could not come apart from the sorrow.

"For you are with me; your rod and your staff they comfort me." The Lord is my Shepherd: I shall not lack perfect comfort in every sorrow from the God of all comfort. The shepherd is with the sheep at every step of the dangerous pathway through the cold, damp valley. His rod and staff keep from stumbling, hold the sheep to the path, and give assurance that the shepherd is near. So the Lord's own presence is with us, giving abundant deliverance, taking away all fear on the one hand, and giving supernatural comfort on the other.

Have you feared concerning the past, or the present, or the future? Do you know that from now until the time you see the Lord face to face He is caring for all the future, so that you need not fear? If you have fear, you have not faith. That is, you do not believe that the Lord is your Shepherd.

As I lay one day in the hospital facing an operation about which the doctors themselves had real uncertainty, I looked to the Lord for some message from his Word. The first sentence that came to my mind was one of the most familiar in the Bible, something that might be thought of as not a new, fresh message: "Yea, though I walk through the valley of the shadow of death, I will fear no evil." Those words, "I will fear no evil," came as the voice from heaven, a direct command that I was not to fear. The thought came: But suppose something should go wrong and the operation result in death? Then came the glad, restful assurance that the Shepherd, the one who has conquered death, is the one whose promises take care of every contingency. His word is absolute: Fear no evil! No evil can come to one who leans on the Shepherd who turns evil into glory.

"You prepare a table before me in the presence of my enemies." The Lord is my Shepherd: I shall not lack victory over Satan and all the power of sin. This undoubtedly is the heart of the message contained in this picture of the shepherd's preparing a table in the presence of the enemies of the sheep. The thought here is not so much the provision of food for the sheep, but the presence of the enemies — the serpents and scorpions, or even the lion and the bear — with the shepherd there to protect the sheep. How often Christians long that Christ should prepare a table in the presence of the angels of God. How often Christians long for a life of pleasantness and blessedness, with congenial friends, comfort without danger. But the miracle of this psalm of resurrection life is the perfect provision in the very midst of the enemy's country.

Satan is the prince of this world, the god of this age. But he is a defeated foe. When our Lord said, "I saw Satan fall like lightning from heaven" (Luke 10:18), he saw in prophetic vision the complete defeat of Satan. The thing that indicated that defeat was the fact that the disciples of the Lord, in his name, had power to cast out demons. When the Holy Spirit comes to us, He convicts the world of judgment, because the prince of this world has been judged (John 16:8-11). The proof that Satan is a defeated foe is that there are men controlled by the Lord Jesus Christ over whom Satan has no power. "he who is in you is greater than he who is in the world" (1 John 4:4).

This victory over the enemy does not mean that we are sinless while we are in this body. It does mean that when we are tempted, or when we are convicted of sin and failure, there is God's provision to give victory at that point by the power of His Spirit.

"You anoint my head with oil; my cup overflows." The Lord is my Shepherd: I shall not want joy and the fullness of life. Christ was anointed with the oil of gladness above his fellows (Psalm 45:7). The anointing symbolizes great gladness, and also indicates power for service. We are to serve the Lord with gladness (Psalm 100:2). Our Shepherd gives joy unspeakable and full of glory, and the fullness of power for service (1 Peter 1:8). The cup running over is a picture of joy and of abundant supply of every need. He has come to give life more abundantly — overflowingly (John 10:10). This prepares the way for the closing cry of triumphant trust:

"Surely goodness and mercy shall follow me all the days of my life." The New Testament parallel to this testimony is in 2 Cor. 2:14, "But thanks be to God, who in Christ always leads us in triumphal procession." Are we reading it, "Goodness and mercy shall follow me every now and then," or, "Goodness and mercy shall follow me most of the days of my life"? Goodness and mercy constitute the grace of our Lord Jesus Christ. Grace is more, infinitely more, than "unmerited favor." It is God's abounding favor toward those who merit the opposite. It includes mercy or loving kindness toward sinners, and it includes "goodness," that is, the supply of every need, for bankrupt lives.

"And I shall dwell in the house of the Lord for ever." As the fourth verse, concerning the valley of the shadow of death, is so often applied to death, so the closing sentence is nearly always applied to heaven. After goodness and mercy follow us all the days of our life, then we dwell in the house of the Lord forever. That is certainly true; and it is a glorious prospect. But the twenty-third Psalm is the Psalm of life, and there is a clear indication that this last sentence does not refer primarily to heaven, or in any case is not to be limited to heaven. In Psalm 27:4 David says, "One thing have I asked of the Lord, that will I seek after: that I may dwell in the house of the Lord all the days of my life, to gaze upon the beauty of the Lord and to inquire in his temple." The twenty-third Psalm is a description of the fullness of blessing to be found in the presence of the Lord as we dwell in His house all the days of our life here, and then continue with increasing joy and fullness unto the ages of the ages. The words "for ever" in this verse mean literally, "unto length of days," and is not one of the words ordinarily used for "forever."

The late Mrs. Field, consecrated leader of Hephzibah House in New York City, often asked the question: "Are you an out-and-out Christian?" Her friend Dr. C. I. Scofield said one day: "Mrs. Field, you never ask me if I am an out-and-out Christian."

"Well, I will ask you now. Are you?"

"No," he answered, and before Mrs. Field recovered from her astonishment, he added: "I am an in-and-out Christian. The Lord's sheep will go in and out and find pasture" (John 10:9). The Shepherd of the twenty-third Psalm is our dwelling place. "Lord, you have been our dwelling place in all generations" (Psalm 90:1). The house of the Lord in the twenty-third Psalm is the secret place of the Most High: "He that dwells in the shelter of the Most High shall abide in the shadow of the Almighty" (Psalm 91:1).

Is not this the Psalm of victorious life? If there should be one that is thus shepherded, is he not one who has every need supplied? Has anything been left out? There is the supply of every spiritual and every material need. The Lord is my shepherd: I shall not want forgiveness, restoration, refreshment, guidance, deliverance from fear, comfort, victory over enemies, the joy of the Lord, power for service, continual abiding in the living Lord, with every step of the journey covered by the abounding grace of the Savior-Shepherd of souls.

Chapter 3

How the Shepherd Does It

Two questions remain concerning this abundant, abounding, resurrection life of the twenty-third Psalm. The first question is: How does God actually accomplish these things, and bring this victory to his children here and now, during their earthly pilgrimage, as they live in the presence of their enemies?

There are two answers to this question. The first answer is found in the twenty-second Psalm. If the "orphan cry" of anguish: "My God, my God, why have you forsaken me?" had never been uttered by the Son or God, then the words, "The Lord is my shepherd: I shall not want," never could have been uttered by any man.

There are those who vainly seek to enter the green pastures of the twenty-third Psalm by some other pathway than the blood-marked way of the twenty-second Psalm. All men want what they call "the abundant life." But they want it without the stumbling-block of the cross. There are religions that seek to persuade men that they may have the peace that passes understanding, the joy unspeakable, and victory over sin and sickness and death, without the paying of the penalty of eternal death that rests upon every sinner. Men of violence cannot rush into the treasure-house of the twenty-third Psalm unless they come by way of the twenty-second. Yet this does not mean that the man himself must go through Gethsemane and suffer on the cross.

"Jesus paid it all." He died in our place. The first step toward enjoying the provision of the Psalm of life is to receive eternal life through faith in the crucified and risen Savior. It is the death and resurrection of Christ set forth in Psalm 22 that make possible for us the Christian life set forth in the twenty-third Psalm.

The blood of Christ purchases for us full salvation. Salvation, past, present, and future, is all of grace. The condition of our salvation is faith, but the *ground* of our righteousness and redemption is the blood of Christ.

The second answer to the question, How does the Shepherd supply our needs? Is, through the Holy Spirit.

When we accept Christ, and the sacrifice he has made for us, we are born of the Spirit, and by the power of the Holy Spirit we are united with Christ. The two sides of God's provision therefore are these: Christ *for us,* and Christ *in us.* Christ died on the cross for us, and rose again for us. Now he lives within us, and this miracle is needed for the supplying of all those needs pictured in the twenty-third Psalm.

All things in creation and in redemption come from God the Father, as the source. All things come through God the Son, as the channel. All things come by God the Holy Spirit, as the agent. God the Father has given all things to the Son (John 3:35; 16:15). Then he gave his Son to us, and with Christ he freely gave us all things (Romans 8:32). The Father and the Son both sent forth the Holy Spirit, whose work in the believer is to take of the things of Christ and make them real in our lives (John 16:13-15).

The twenty-third Psalm, therefore, is a beautiful picture or figure, in terms of the shepherd and the sheep, of the Lord Jesus providing every need through the power of the Spirit. The victorious life is the Spirit-filled life. Our Lord said, "If anyone thirsts, let him come to me and drink. Whoever believes in me, as the Scripture has said, 'Out of his heart will flow rivers of living water.'" Now this he said about the

Spirit, whom those who believed in him were to receive, for as yet the Spirit had not been given, because Jesus was not yet glorified" (John 7:37-39).

Now, Jesus *has* been glorified. The Spirit has been given; he is the living water. Our Lord said, as recorded in Matthew, "If you then, who are evil, know how to give good gifts to your children, how much more will your Father who is in heaven give good things to those who ask him?" (Matt. 7:11). These are the good things of the twenty-third Psalm: "I shall not want any good thing." As the saying is recorded in Luke (referring to another occasion), our Lord says: "how much more will the heavenly Father give the Holy Spirit to those who ask him!" (Luke 11:13). The way he gives us good things is by giving us Christ, and with Christ giving us all things, then by giving us the Holy Spirit, who takes these things of Christ and makes them real in our lives. Our Lord gave us his joy and his peace. The fruit of the Spirit is joy and peace.

The Shepherd restores our souls by the Holy Spirit. He forgives and cleanses us as Christians. He gives life to our mortal bodies, by his Spirit, who dwells in us (Rom. 8:11-13). He sends forth his Spirit of truth to lead us in the paths of righteousness. The Spirit is truly called, "Comforter," though the word "Paraclete" (one called to be alongside) includes much more than comfort. The anointing that we have is the anointing of the Holy Spirit. The fruit of the Spirit is simply another expression of the blessings of the twenty-third Psalm. "The fruit of the Spirit is love," and then follow four pairs of twins, love's children, so to speak; joy and peace, long-suffering and kindness, goodness and faithfulness, meekness and self-control (Gal. 5:22, 23).

We, as we live in our bodies, are incapable of righteousness. But God gives life to our mortal bodies through the Holy Spirit who dwells in us (Rom. 8:11). That is, he gives spiritual life, making us capable of doing righteousness.

"How beautiful! Can you do it?" These were the words of an intelligent Chinese man who heard for the first time a message on the Christian life. Our second question is, "How may we enter into the victory so fully provided by God?" This brings us back to our first question concerning the twenty-third Psalm, "Do you believe it?"

Chapter 4

How We Enter In

We have considered first the riches of God's provision for victorious living as presented in the twenty-third Psalm. We have discovered that such provision is the costliest thing in the world. The cost is the precious blood of Christ. It costs also the mighty power of God. Redemption is through blood and through power, through death and resurrection. The measure of God's power in the Old Testament is his power in creating the universe. The measure of his power in the New Testament is the exceeding greatness of his power which he wrought in Christ when he raised him from the dead. The resurrection power of Christ is expressed in the mighty working of the Holy Spirit in regeneration, and in sanctification, as he supplies every need of the believer.

But if it is true that all things come from God the Father, and all things come through God the Son, and all things come by the Holy Spirit, how is it that Christians, indwelt by the Holy Spirit, are so often defeated and discouraged, fearing evil, in sadness, and often in despair? Surely it is not because of God's lack of provision. Surely it is not because God is a respecter of persons, and gives joy to one Christian but withholds from another. What is the thing that the Christian must do to enter into the victory of the twenty-third Psalm?

Every true Christian has the supply of riches of the twenty-third Psalm. Why is he not enjoying it? There are just two things that can keep a Christian from enjoying Christ's abundant provision for him in the present moment. One is the failure to yield himself unto God. If there is something he is consciously holding back, then he has a controversy with the Lord, and cannot know the joy and peace that are his until he yields. But a large number of Christians have yielded to the utmost of their conscious thought. They would hold nothing back from the Lord. They would be ready to die for him. Yet they are, like Martha, anxious and troubled about many things. They have not found the secret of the one thing that is needful, the blessing of the twenty-third Psalm. The reason is, they do not believe the twenty-third Psalm.

Now we shall face this fact in a very practical and direct way. There are many Christians who feel that faith is a subtle something that must in a mysterious way be given to them, and that they have no responsibility in the matter. One of the ways in which God gives us faith is to give us the twenty-third Psalm and ask us to accept it.

Face now the question personally and earnestly: "Do you believe that the Lord is your shepherd?" Nearly every Christian will answer at once, "Of course I do."

Many years ago, Charles G. Trumbull, editor of the *Sunday School Times,* was giving messages on the victorious Christian life. A minister who was present, a man of great gifts and of unusual success in the ministry, came to Dr. Trumbull for an interview. He confessed that he was defeated. He was hungry for something that he did not have in his Christian life. After these two men talked together for a time, the layman asked the minister: "Do you believe the first verse of the twenty-third Psalm?"

"Of course I do. I have often preached on that text. It is one of my favorite texts."

"What kind of a shepherd is Jesus Christ? Does he supply some of the needs of the sheep, or all of the needs of the sheep?"

"Why — yes, of course, he supplies all the needs of the sheep."

The minister hesitated in his answer. He saw where his admission was leading him. Dr. Trumbull said, "Now look out! You are putting yourself into a corner, and it is the most blessed corner you ever got into in your life."

The conversation ended with the two men on their knees, and the minister for the first time in his life clearly and consciously believed the statement: "The Lord is my Shepherd." That is, he had not been believing that Christ was supplying all his needs. Do you believe it?

There are hundreds, perhaps thousands of Christians, who have been led out of defeat into victory, out of discouragement and worry into joy and peace and rest, by recognizing that they were not believing the first verse of the twenty-third Psalm: "The Lord is my Shepherd."

A missionary who had been used in a remarkable way as a soul-winner, came on one of her furloughs to a conference in America, where seven years before she had heard the message of victory in Christ. For seven years she had been hungry and thirsty for victory and joy and peace, and for the solution of many problems in her life and in her home. She longed to come back to that conference center, thinking that she might there learn the secret. She read many splendid books on the Spirit-filled life; she knew the truth, but was burdened and defeated in her life. She visited those conference grounds for a few days unexpectedly. I attended a meeting in which this missionary gave a thrilling presentation of the work in Africa. At the close of the meeting in a personal interview she poured out her heart in a narrative of defeat and longing for victory. At the close, she said, "I know what my trouble is. It is unbelief." She had diagnosed her case. She knew all the teachings about the Spirit-filled life. She knew what she needed to do. But she was anxious and troubled and defeated.

"Do you believe the first verse of the twenty-third Psalm?"

"'The Lord is my Shepherd.' Certainly I do."

"How long have you believed it?"

"Ever since I became a Christian."

"Were you believing it five minutes ago?"

"Of course I was."

"What does a shepherd do?"

"He guides the sheep and meets their needs."

"Does that statement then mean that the Lord Jesus Christ is meeting all our needs? Is he meeting all your needs?"

"He will if I let him."

"That does not answer the question. This statement is that the Lord Jesus Christ is meeting all your needs. Is he meeting all your needs?"

"He is doing his part."

"That is perfectly true. But you have not answered the question. Is the Lord meeting all your needs?"

"I have never worried about any of my material needs. The Lord has provided in a wonderful way."

"But are your material needs your greatest needs? Do you not have spiritual needs that the Shepherd must supply?"

"Yes, indeed. The material needs are the smallest part of it. No, the Lord is not meeting my needs."

"But you said that you believe that the Lord is your Shepherd, and that means that the Lord is meeting all your needs."

"Well, I suppose I believe it with my head, but not with my heart."

"Do not get tangled by that distinction. The only way you can believe this statement is with your mind. You do not believe it with your mind. It is a statement of fact that Christ is meeting your need, and you do not believe it. You think that you have evidence that he is not meeting your need, and so you are looking to that evidence, and you are not believing what God says."

"Well, tell me what is the matter, I always thought that I believed it."

"You are saying with your lips that you believe. But you have not given its real meaning to that sentence. James writes, "if someone says he has faith but does not have works? Can that faith save him?" No, because it is not faith. It is just a man's saying he has faith. Now, understand, you as a Christian in a sense do believe that the Lord is your Shepherd. You trust the Lord to meet many of your needs. But you do not believe the plain statement that Christ is meeting *all* of your needs."

She saw the simplicity of it, and then she simply accepted the word of God that the Lord was meeting all her needs.

"Do you now believe that the Lord is your Shepherd?" I asked.

"Yes."

"How do you know?"

"Just because he says so."

"How long have you believed it?"

"I have just now seen it."

We knelt together, and after seven years of being anxious and troubled and struggling for victory, this devoted missionary thanked God that the Lord was her Shepherd. With none of the outward circumstances changed, she arose with peace in her heart, and thanksgiving that God was meeting every need.

A day or two later the missionary said that when she was considering whether she believed the twenty-third Psalm with her heart or with her mind, she did not at that time recall a striking expression used by the native Christians in Africa. "When they speak of a professing Christian who gives no evidence of the power of God in his life, they never say, 'He is a head-believer'; they say, 'He is a lip-believer.'" And so we also may say, "The Lord is my Shepherd," and be saying it with our lips, without giving its true meaning to the statement. That statement is a fact, not a promise, although the fact includes in it all the promises of God, which are yea and amen in Christ.

If we have taken Christ as our Savior, we are the sheep of his pasture. He is our Shepherd. He is supplying all our needs. Our faith does not make this true. We believe it because it is true. If we go forward without believing it, we do not change the fact, but we do change greatly the enjoyment of our rich possessions in Christ. Faith is the victory. That is, faith lays hold of him who is the victory. Our faith is the condition of receiving Christ as our Savior; so also, walking by faith is the condition of present victory.

When this simple truth in all its bright glory comes first to our minds and hearts, there is indeed a transformation. There is a crisis of entering into the meaning of living by the power of the Holy Spirit. This crisis includes our complete yielding to Christ, just as the sheep hear the voice of the shepherd and follow him, and then fully trusting the Shepherd.

We have thought of the Shepherd as the one who is meeting all our needs, and the one who is leading his sheep (Ps. 80.1). But the Leader is the Lord. The Provider is the Prince. God said to David: "You shall be shepherd of my people Israel, and you shall be prince over Israel" (2 Sam. 5:2). David was their shepherd to guide and to rule (Ps. 78:70-72). So the Messiah, of whom David was the type, is the Shepherd and the Prince (Eze. 34:23, 24); he is the Shepherd and the Ruler (Mic. 5:2-4). So our Shepherd is our Lord, to whom we must yield implicit obedience.

The difference between defeat and victory is the difference between the position of the word "but." We ask, "Do you believe that the Lord is your Shepherd?" "Yes, *but…*" That fatal word "but" shows that we do not believe that the Lord is our Shepherd. "Yes, I believe it, *but* I do not have victory over my bad temper; I am not able to see people come to faith in Christ; I worry about things; I do not have peace and joy." The testimony of victory puts "but" into the right place. "I am passing through a time of great sorrow and trouble, *but* the Lord is my Shepherd." "I have been discouraged about my past accomplishments, *but* the Lord is my Shepherd." "I have great weaknesses along this line, or that, *but* the Lord is my Shepherd." So Paul: "my spirit was not at rest … *But* thanks be to God, who in Christ always leads us in triumphal procession" (2 Cor. 2:13, 14).

Chapter 5

How We Continue

This crisis of surrender and faith is followed by a process. The path of righteousness does not always lead beside the still waters, or in the green pastures of rest, but also goes through the valley of deep darkness, and into the midst of powerful and terrible enemies. It is not an experience of "the victorious life," or any other kind of experience, that is the secret of victory. It is the Shepherd constantly with us who is himself the victory. As we receive Christ Jesus, so we are to walk in him. As we see the glory of putting our trust in the Shepherd, so we are to apply that truth step by step. He feeds us with the living bread and gives us the water of life. But we are to feed diligently upon the written Word as our bread, and drink of the living water of God's Spirit.

This life of victory is not perfection in the sense of sinlessness, nor in the sense of complete maturity. In one sense we do have a perfect heart toward our Shepherd. This is expressed in surrender and trust. The difference in the life of defeat and victory is not that there are no sins or failures for the Christian who has learned the secret of the twenty-third Psalm. But it is that we put to death "the doings of the body" by the power of the Spirit, through faith, not in our own strength. When we sin, we confess and the Shepherd restores our soul, which means both forgiveness and power for victory at that very place of failure.

We have seen that all things come from God the Father as the source. All things come from God the Son as the channel. All things come by God the Holy Spirit as the agent. The Father has given all things to his Son. He has given his Son to us, and with his Son he has freely given us all things. The Holy Spirit makes them real to us. But it is also true that all these things, these treasures of the twenty-third Psalm, come to us by faith, and in answer to prayer.

When we pray "Give us this day our daily bread," we pray in faith because the Lord is our Shepherd, leading us in green pastures and by still waters. He supplies our daily bread, meets our every need. Yet He would be inquired of us, that He may do this thing. We pray, "Forgive us our debts, as we forgive our debtors." The Lord is our Shepherd; he restores our souls, forgiving our sins and cleansing our hearts.

We pray, "Lead us not into temptation." This is another way of praying that the Lord would lead us in right paths. He is our Shepherd and leads us into paths of righteousness. We pray, "Deliver us from the evil one." He is our Shepherd; he sets the table before us in the presence of our enemies, and protects us from their attacks.

Thus is the glory of salvation by grace, through faith, revealed. The Lord Jesus is meeting all our needs. He does one hundred percent of all that he alone can do. We are to do one hundred percent of all that we by his grace, have to do. The life of resting in the finished work of Christ, and in the present mighty working of Christ, is not a life of passivity. It is the life set free for true activity. Shall we begin to live it? We have been saved by our Shepherd. We have surrendered to our Shepherd. Now we trust and serve our Shepherd.

A little child had difficulty memorizing the first verse of the twenty-third Psalm and she finally got it this way: "The Lord is my Shepherd: that's all I want." If we know the Shepherd, that is all we need or want. For this is life victorious, to know the Shepherd, who is meeting every need.

"The LORD is my Shepherd."

"The Lord IS my Shepherd."

"The Lord is MY Shepherd."

"The Lord is my SHEPHERD."

About the Author

Robert C. McQuilkin was the first president of Columbia International University from 1923-1952. In 1918, McQuilkin and his wife Marguerite were days away from an assignment as missionaries when the ship that was to carry them to Africa burned and sunk the day before the ship's departure. That left McQuilkin questioning God's next move for him and opened up the opportunity for McQuilkin to later accept the position to lead a new work in Columbia, South Carolina, called the Southern Bible Institute. It would soon be renamed Columbia Bible College, and by 1994, Columbia International University.

After earning a bachelor's degree from the University of Pennsylvania, McQuilkin began working in 1912 as associate editor for the influential *Sunday School Times*. It was during this period that McQuilkin established the Oxford Conference in Pennsylvania where he proclaimed the "Victorious Christian Life" message, which would become a core value of CIU.

In conjunction with CIU, McQuilkin founded the Ben Lippen Conference Center, a place where the Victorious Christian Life was proclaimed and where young people were encouraged to consider the mission field.

During his ministry, McQuilkin spoke widely and authored a number of books including, *The Lord is My Shepherd, Let Not Your Heart be Troubled, Victory in Christ,* and *Joy and Victory.*

CIU

**Columbia
International
University**

Columbia International University exists to
train men and women from a biblical world
view to impact the nations with the message
of Christ through service in the marketplace,
missions and the local church.

For more information about undergraduate,
graduate and seminary programs at
Columbia International University, visit
www.ciu.edu

Made in the USA
Monee, IL
27 June 2020